William Bolcom

Four Preludes
on Jewish Melodies

for organ

(2005)

ISBN-13: 978-1-4234-2885-5
ISBN-10: 1-4234-2885-4

EDWARD B. MARKS MUSIC COMPANY / Exclusively Distributed By HAL•LEONARD® CORPORATION
7777 W. BLUEMOUND RD. P.O. BOX 13819 MILWAUKEE, WI 53213

www.ebmarks.com
www.halleonard.com

Commissioned by the Tangeman Sacred Music Center
of the College-Conservatory of Music,
University of Cincinnati

I. Hinei Mah Tov

II. Yism'chu

III. Hal'luhu

IV. Sim Shalom

I. HINEI MAH TOV
traditional

Hi - nei mah tov u - mah na - im she - vet a - chim gam ya - chad

Hi - nei mah___ tov she - vet a - chim gam ya - chad.

How good it is, and how pleasant, when we dwell together in unity.

II. YISM'CHU
folktune

Yis - m' -chu b' - ma -l' chu - t' -cha sho -m' -rei, sho -m' rei,

sho - m' -rei sha - bat v' - ko - r' -ei o - neg___ sha - bat, sha - bat.

1.Am___ m' - ka - d' shei,___ m' - ka - d'-shei sh' -vi - i,___ sha - bat,
2.U -vash' vi - i___ ra - tzi - ta bo,___ ra - tzi - ta bo v' -ki - dash to, sha - bat,
3.Zei - cher___ l' - ma - a - sei___ l' - ma - a - sei v' -rei - sheet, sha - bat,

ku - lam yis - b' - u___ v' - yit -an' -gu - mi - tu - ve - cha, sha - bat.
chem - dat ya - mim___ o - to___ ka - ra - ta,___ sha - bat.
zei - cher l' - ma - a - sei,___ l' - ma - a - sei v' -rei - sheet,_ sha - bat.

Those who keep the Sabbath and call it a delight shall rejoice in Your deliverance.
All who hallow the seventh day shall be gladdened by Your goodness.
This day is Israel's festival of the spirit, sanctified and blessed by You,
the most precious of days, a symbol of the joy of creation.

III. HAL'LUHU
folksong

Ha - l' -lu -hu, ha - l' -lu -hu b' - tzil - tz' -lei sha - ma, ha - l' -lu -hu,

ha - l' -lu -hu b' - tzil - tz' -lei t'ru - ah, kol han' -sha -mah t' - ha -leil Yah, ha - l' -lu - yah,

ha - l' - lu - yah,___ kol han' -sha -mah t' - ha -leil Yah, ha - l' -lu - yah, ha - l' -lu - yah.

Praise God with resounding cymbals, praise God with loud-sounding cymbals.
Let all that breathe praise the Lord. Halleluyah!

IV. SIM SHALOM
Chassidic folksong

Refrain:

Sim sha -lom to - vah uv' -ra -cha chein va -che -sed v'-

ra -cha -mim, v' -ra -cha -mim a - lei - nu v' - al kol Yis -ra -eil, v' - al kol Yis -ra -eil a - me -cha.

1.Ba -r' -chei - nu a - vi -nu ku -la -nu k' -e -chad b' -or pa -ne - cha,
2.To - rat__ cha - yim v'a -ha -vat__ che - sed v' - a -ha -vat che - sed utz' da
3.V' - tov__ b' -ei -nei -cha__ l' - va - reich____ et am -cha Yis -ra -eil b'-

D.S. al Coda   *Coda*

ki -b' -or pa -ne -cha na -ta -ta la - nu A -do -nai e -lo -hei - nu.   a - me -cha.
ka__ uv' -ra chah__ v' -ra - cha -mim v' -cha -yim v' - sha - lom.
chol_____ eit u -v' -chol sha - ah_____ bish' -lo -me - cha.

Peace, happiness, and blessing; grace and love and mercy: may these descend on us, on all Israel, and all the world.
Bless us, our Creator, one and all, with the light of Your presence; for by that light, O God, You have revealed to us
the law of life: to love kindness and justice and mercy, to seek blessing, life, and peace. O bless Your people Israel
and all peoples with enduring peace! Blessed are You, Lord, who blesses Your people Israel with peace.

ACCIDENTALS

N.B. Accidentals obtain throughout a beamed group. Unbeamed notes within a measure continue the same accidental until interrupted by another note or rest. (Additional courtesy accidentals are given to ensure clarity.) In music with key signatures, traditional rules apply.

Optional Crotales for III. Hal'luhu
(to be played by a separate performer)

The indicated pitches (sounding *8va*)
should be mounted on a board

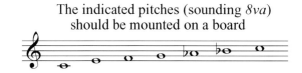

FOUR PRELUDES
ON JEWISH MELODIES

I. Hinei Mah Tov

WILLIAM BOLCOM

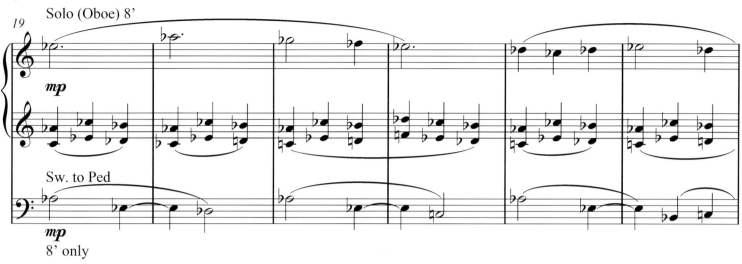

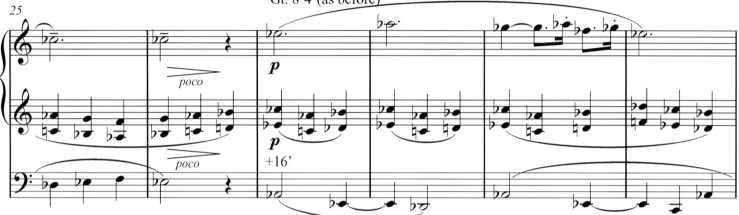

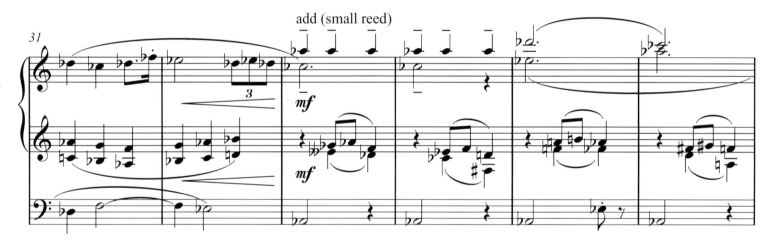

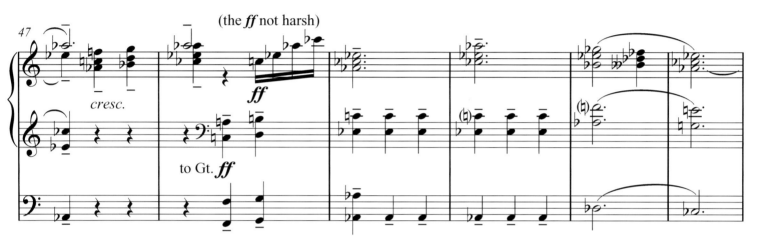

II. Yism'chu

Stately but moving forward ($\bullet$ = 96)

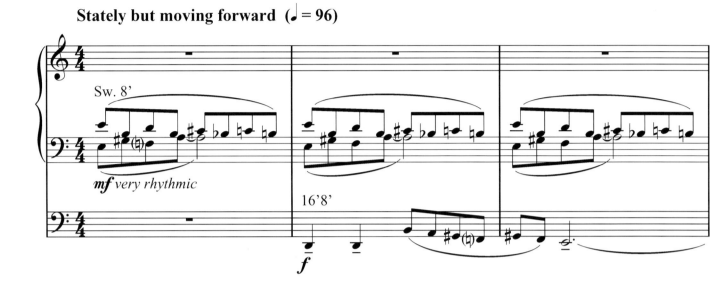

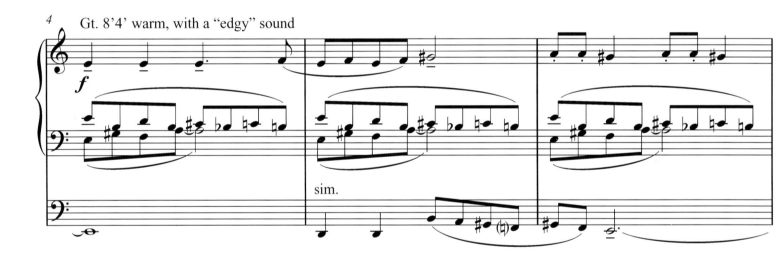

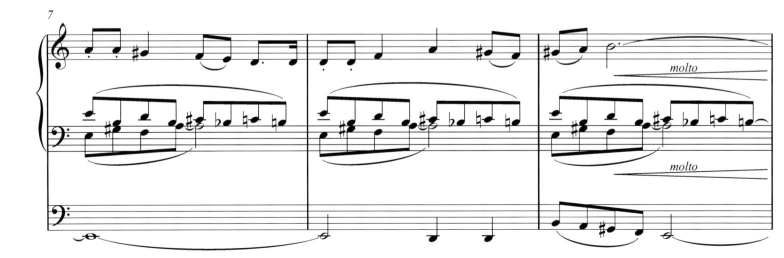

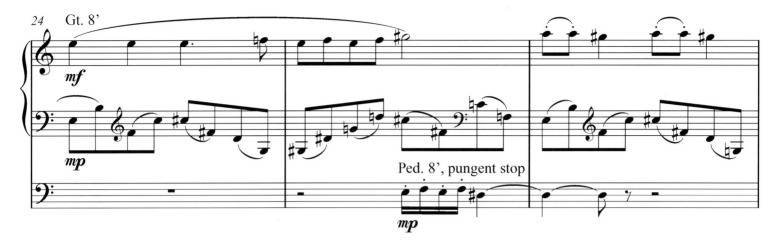

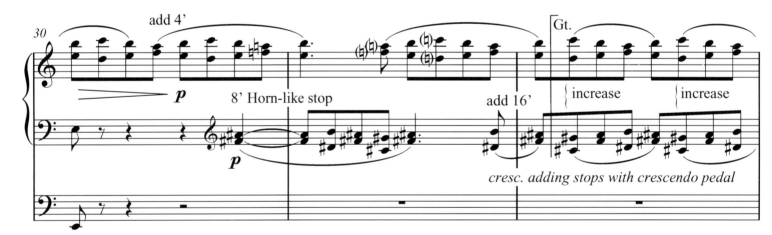

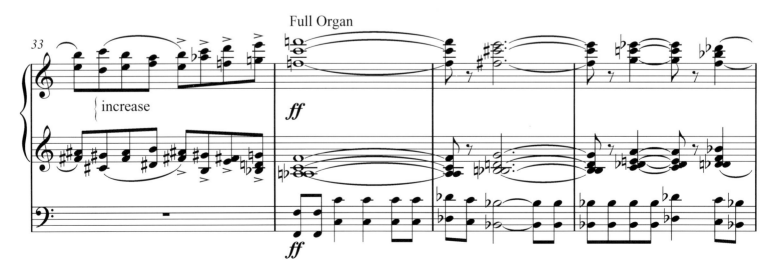

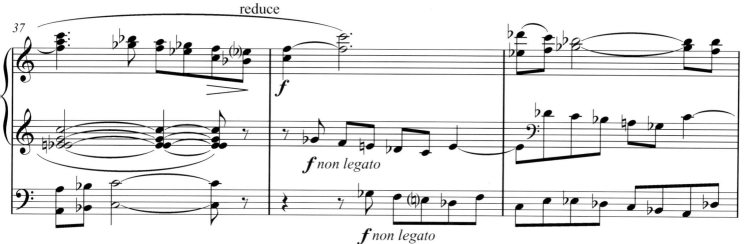

* trattenuto: a *very* slight ritard.

A shade slower; *simple, meditative*

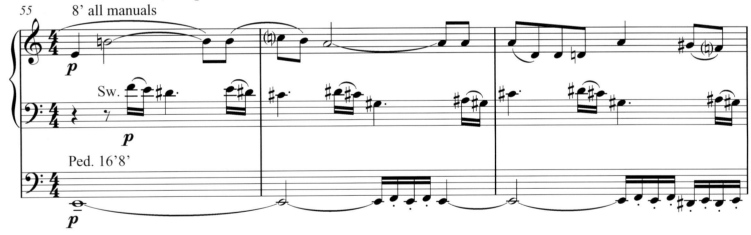

III. Hal'luhu

♩. = 66, *with a solemn lilt,* very strict in tempo

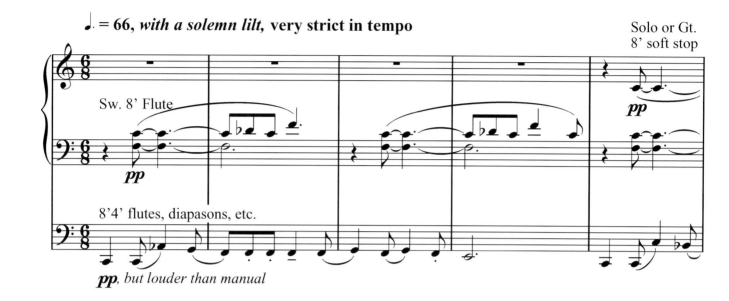

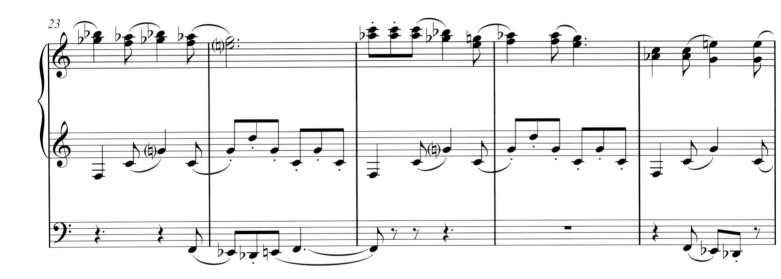

CROTALES (optional—see p.6)

attacca

IV. Sim Shalom

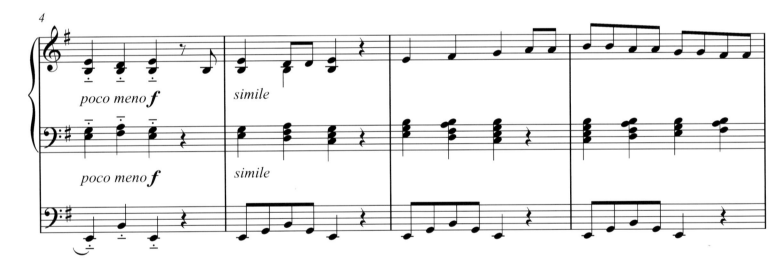

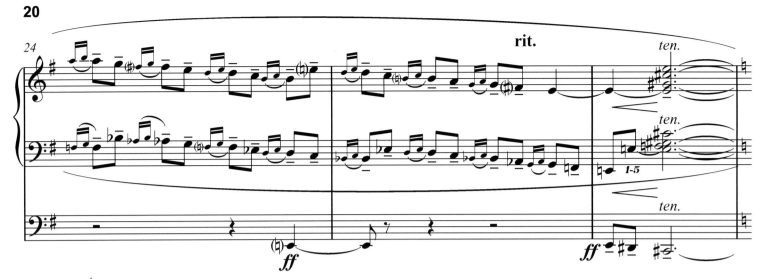

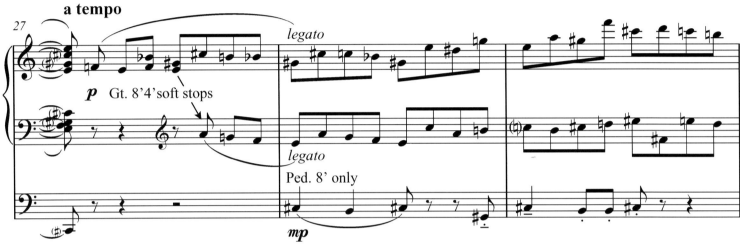

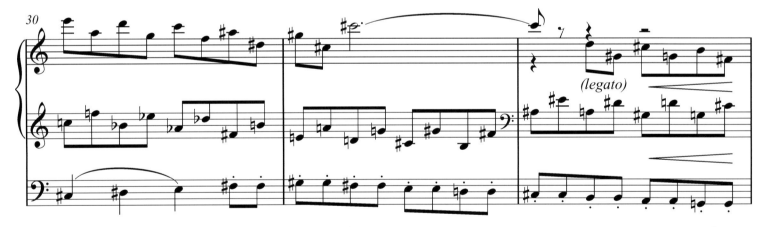

A little faster

tratt.

add stops

a tempo primo

not quite Full Organ

accel.

Più agitato

allarg.

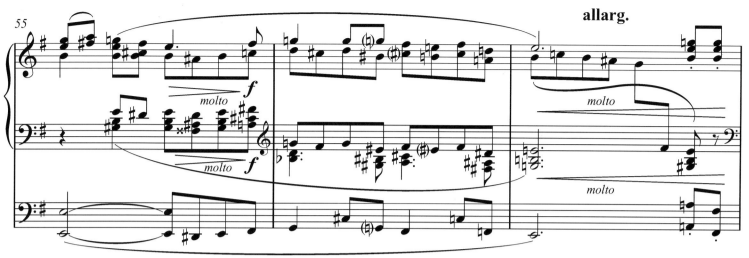

Broader
Full Organ

slower and slower to end

Very slow

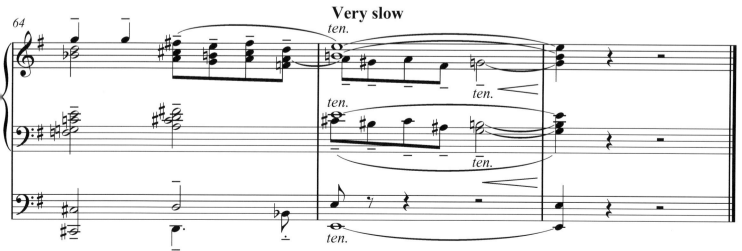